FACE TO FACE WITH
WHALES

by Flip & Linda Nicklin

NATIONAL
GEOGRAPHIC

WASHINGTON, D.C.

◄ I have been very lucky to spend my life with whales and the people who study them. My wife, Linda, is my partner in whale watching and in writing this book.

FACE TO FACE

The first time I slipped into the water with a singing humpback whale, I was not thinking about how it would change my life. I was just gazing at the motionless dark shape below me and feeling my bones hum with the sounds it was making. I tried to quiet my excited breathing so I could dive down to take the whale's picture.

◄ The eye of a humpback whale is as big as a dinner plate and its pupil is as big as an orange.

I could hear the strange loud moans, trills, and gurgles that make up the humpback "song"

5

➡ *We usually hold our breath to go underwater and photograph a whale. The whale has to help by being willing to stay near us. They are better swimmers than we are.*

SEA MONSTERS

People have always told stories about monsters that live in the sea. Some of these tales were probably inspired by whales. Here's what makes whales like sea monsters:

▬ Up close, a whale can seem as big as an island.

▬ They can appear right next to your boat, then suddenly disappear.

▬ They make strange sounds.

▬ A whale may swim under a boat and bump it.

before I even left the boat. In the water, the whale's song was so loud that my whole body was vibrating.

It was a spring day in 1979. Until that day, we didn't know that we could get close to singing whales and watch them while they sang. Then scientist Jim Darling looked through the surface of the water where he had just seen a whale dive. He could see something down below. It turned out to be the whale. It had stopped swimming and was hanging motionless, singing. I was in a boat nearby, and they called me over to photograph it.

It was thrilling to photograph a scientific breakthrough as it was happening. We had discovered that we could find these singing whales and that they became still and kept singing. With my mask and snorkel and camera, I could watch and record them. We could learn more about who

these whales were and what they did and maybe even figure out exactly why they sang.

When I got in the water that day, my love of photography and my childhood dream of being a scientist came together. I would go on to photograph many kinds of whales in many places. But I kept going back to Hawaii, where I first saw that singing whale, to work with Jim Darling and help him learn more about humpback whale behavior.

This humpback whale is singing into our underwater microphone. These whales sing the longest and most complex songs of any animal. Songs may be 10–20 minutes long.

MEET

Smaller and sleeker than the other great whales, minkes are about 26 feet (8 m) long and weigh 6 to 8 tons (5,400-8,100 kg). Minkes are fast swimmers and eat a variety of foods. They are one of a few species still being hunted.

THE WHALE

With their snow white skin and thick blubber, belugas are well adapted to their life near northern ice. In the Canadian Arctic, one beluga came up to look at me. Then it left and returned with about 35 friends. Good thing they're so friendly looking!

When I was a boy, my family used to watch whales from the coast near San Diego. All we saw from shore were puffs of mist in the distance. We were actually looking at their breath. These were gray whales, making their way down the coast between summer feeding areas in Canada and Alaska and winter grounds in Baja California. I probably didn't know that at the time. To me they were just smoky puffs near the horizon, distant and mysterious.

The fin whale's 1 lower jaw is white on one side and dark on the other. Right whales 2 weigh about 55 tons, but eat tiny plankton. Pilot whales 3 live in every ocean except the Arctic Ocean. Humpbacks 4 often leap from the water or slap their tails or fins on the surface. The narwhal 5 has been called the "unicorn of the sea" because of its long spiraled tusk. The sperm whale 6 can dive thousands of feet and stay down for over an hour.

Their breath was a clue that these animals are not fish. Whales are mammals. They breathe air like we do. Females give birth to live babies and nurse them on their milk. They even have a few hairs.

There are many kinds, or species, of whale. The biggest whale is also the biggest animal that ever lived on Earth, the blue whale. It can be 90 feet (27 m) long and can weigh between 90-150 tons (81,600-136,000 kg), as much as 30 elephants. The dwarf sperm whale is the smallest. It is less than ten feet (3.1 m) long.

Whales live in every ocean in the world. Different species of whales live in different areas and eat different diets. Humpback whales are familiar to people because these whales live close to the coast. Whales such as the bottlenose and beaked whales are hardly known, because they live in the deep ocean. Some whales—like bowheads, narwhals, and belugas—live in far northern seas. Some make long migrations, or journeys, across the Earth's oceans each year. Others live most of their lives in one area.

Whales are well designed for their ocean lifestyles. They have thick layers of blubber under

Whales evolved from hoofed, meat-eating land animals. Their closest land relatives are hippos, cows, and deer. As whales adapted to life in the sea, their nostrils moved to the tops of their heads, they lost their hind limbs, and their front limbs became flippers.

WHALE ANCESTOR

BALEEN WHALES

TOOTHED WHALES

WHALE COUSINS

their skin that keep them warm even in very cold water. They are speedy swimmers and can move through the water with little effort, especially considering how big they are.

While hunting for food, whales have to hold their breath. Luckily, they take in more air in one breath than land animals can, and their blood is better at moving and storing oxygen, so they don't have to breathe as often. They can also catch lots of food at once. A humpback whale can take in 500 gallons (1,900 liters) of water and prey in one mouthful. A blue whale can eat up to eight tons (7,000 kg) of food in a day.

A photograph taken from an airplane shows an 18-foot (5.5 m) research boat and a much larger blue whale. These whales are the biggest animals on Earth. They are also the loudest, at times making calls that can be heard across an entire ocean.

LIVES

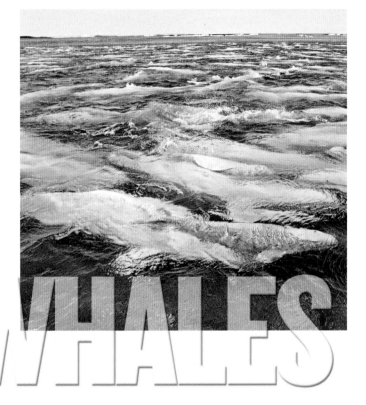

OF WHALES

Belugas like to be close to other belugas and sometimes travel in groups of more than a thousand. They communicate with squeaks, squeals, chirps, barks, whistles, or moans, which is why they were once called "sea canaries."

In this whale pod, the big sperm whale on the left is a male that has been away from the others for years. The smaller ones are females and younger sperm whales. It looks like a family reunion!

It isn't easy to study whales. Except for brief visits to the surface, whales live their lives underwater, and they can be hard to find in the vast oceans.

I spend a lot of time in small boats, waiting for whales or looking for them, without seeing much. But sometimes a whale gets curious and comes close to get a better look. That's when I see and, if I am lucky, photograph their natural behavior. This happened one time with sperm whales off the coast of Dominica, in the Caribbean. I was with

▲ *A young blue whale weighs around two tons (2,700 kg) and is 23 to 27 feet (7-8 m) long when it is born. For the seven to eight months it is nursing, its mother's rich milk will help it gain eight pounds per hour.*

researcher Jonathan Gordon in his boat *Song of the Whale.* We had been watching small groups of female whales and their young, and seeing the occasional big male. But we had not seen these large males and females together until one day, when we saw a group of sperm whales swimming closely around a big male.

Male sperm whales leave their family groups when they are young. Often, they do not return for 20 years. How, we wondered, would the other whales interact with the male? The whales rubbed up against each other with apparent affection. It looked like a joyous reunion.

Whales have one baby at a time, and moms and babies may stay together a year or more. The mother teaches its young to avoid predators and to forage for food. In some species, moms and babies all swim together, forming a "nursery group." These groups share childcare, and the young whales learn together. In every species, whale mothers seem to be patient and protective of their young. They often touch. Young whales swim very close to their moms, where the stream of water pushed by her body helps pull them through the water.

HOW TO EAT LIKE A WHALE

Most of the biggest whale species don't have teeth. Instead, they have long fringes called baleen. These whales squeeze the water out through the baleen and capture their food inside.

Imagine taking a giant mouthful of cereal and milk. If you closed your teeth and squeezed the milk out, trapping the cereal inside, you would be eating like a baleen whale.

An adult humpback whale can eat a ton of food in a day. That's like eating 8,000 fish sandwiches!

There are two main types of whale, and each has a different way to catch food. One type of whale doesn't have teeth. Instead they have something called baleen attached to the roofs of their mouths. Baleen is made of the same substance as fingernails. It hangs in fringed plates, kind of like a bristly moustache inside their mouths. This type of whale will eat by taking in a big gulp of small animals along with a lot of seawater, then partly closing its mouth and squeezing the water out while trapping the prey inside. Some baleen whales have pleats on their throats. They can expand to take in tons of prey and seawater.

Blue, fin, minke, sei, Bryde's, and humpback whales are all baleen whales. Right whales and bowheads are also baleen whales. They eat everything from small fish to krill, which are shrimp-like animals that are found in large quantities in the ocean. Gray whales are baleen whales too.

⬆ *When a whale leaps out of the water and falls back with a loud smacking sound, it is called "breaching." They might be playing, scratching themselves, or showing off.*

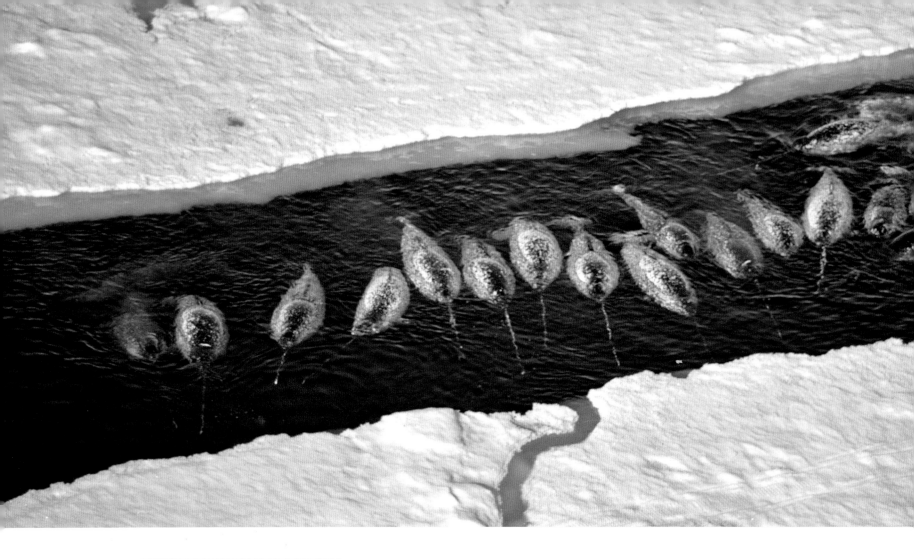

➡ *Each whale's fluke, or tail, is distinctive. In fact, you can identify whole species based on the shape of their flukes. Scientists can even identify some individual whales, such as humpbacks, by their unique tails.*

BLUE WHALE   HUMPBACK WHALE   RIGHT WHALE   SPERM WHALE   GRAY WHALE

These tusked narwhals are resting in open water between sheets of sea ice. It is spring in the high Arctic, and they are waiting for an ice-free passage to open up so they can travel.

These whales often feed along the muddy ocean bottom, sucking up small animals along with a lot of mud, sand, and water. Then they squeeze out most of the muddy water. They must not mind a little dirt in their food!

The other kind of whale has teeth instead of baleen. It usually hunts larger prey, such as fish or squid. Toothed whales include the sperm whale, beluga, and narwhal. Some of the smaller and less well known whales, like the beaked whales and pygmy sperm whales, are also toothed whales. To help them catch food, these whales "echolocate," which means they send out sounds that bounce off objects in their environment. They can read the echoes coming back to get a very complete picture of what is around them in the ocean, even when they can't see because it is so dark down there.

IT'S

We call curious whales "friendlies." Are we studying the whales, or are the whales studying us?

ABOUT THE OCEAN

Oceans have to stay healthy for whales to be healthy. Anything that hurts their food supply, such as pollution, overfishing, or changing ocean temperatures, can be a threat to whales. Whales use sound to communicate with each other and even to find food. Noise caused by human activity can disturb or harm whales.

Whales can be hurt or killed when they are struck by a ship or entangled in fishing gear. In the past, hunting was the most dangerous threat to

Gray whales were sometimes aggressive toward boats in the days when they were hunted. Today, they occasionally approach small boats with gentle intent, wanting to be touched by people. This is an experience these people will never forget!

Where there are healthy oceans with lots of fish, krill, and other animals, you will find whales.

the survival of whales. Some species were caught until their populations were on the brink of extinction. Today, most nations obey an international agreement not to hunt whales. Where they are protected, the populations of some species that were almost extinct are now recovering. Other whale populations are still very endangered.

Attitudes about whales are changing. Many people didn't know much about them and were afraid of them. Now, movies, television, books, and magazine articles have educated people, and they have come to care about whales. Some folks on whale-watching tours have even had personal experiences with whales. It is easy to be fascinated when you have seen them be themselves in their watery world.

If they grab your imagination and interest, you too might grow to love these magnificent creatures and the oceans they swim in. And that will be a good thing—for the oceans, for the whales, and for you!

HOW YOU CAN HELP

Many people are interested in protecting whales because they are such interesting animals. But whales are threatened by some human activities. Here's how you can help:

▬ The water in a stream, creek, or river near you will eventually end up in the ocean. If there is a lot of trash in this waterway, you can join a group that is helping to clean it up.

▬ Ask your parents not to use toxic chemicals on the lawn, and don't throw toxic things like some paints, motor oil, and batteries in the garbage or down the drain. Call your town or city's sanitation department or visit their Web site to find out what to do with harmful household waste. Also, recycle all the aluminum, glass, and newspaper that your family uses. Take bags with you when you go shopping so the cashier doesn't need to give you new bags. Every little bit helps!

▬ You can adopt a whale through the Whale Center of New England (www.whale center.org/adopt.htm), the Whale and Dolphin Adoption Project (www.adopt-a-dolphin.com), or Save the Whales (www.savethe whales.org /adopt.html). These groups study and work to protect whales. When you adopt a whale, you will get pictures of your whale and information about the whale.

▬ You can help by educating yourself and others. Do a school project on the special adaptations—such as baleen and echolocation—that whales have to help them live in the ocean and find food. Or your project could focus on the human activities that threaten whales.

▬ Keep reading about whales and dolphins, and share what you learn with your family and friends.

⬇ *A big whale, a small boat, and cold water can be a frightening combination! This researcher was relieved when the bowhead whale gently set him down again.*

IT'S YOUR TURN

1 First, do some research. Using the Internet, you can listen to whale songs and discover where whales live *(see Find Out More, page 30)*. See which whales live closest to where you live and what they sound like.

2 Next, plan your whale-watching adventure. Is there an aquarium you can visit to see a killer whale or beluga? Or a whale-watching boat you can go on near your home or while you are on vacation?

3 Read about the whales you are likely to see on the adventure you have planned. Make a list of behaviors you will watch for. If you are watching humpbacks, for example, you might see breathing, diving, feeding, lobtailing, pectoral fin slapping, spyhopping, or breaching.

4 When you see whales, write notes or keep a journal page of the different behaviors you see. Don't forget to write down the place you are watching them, and the time and date. Now you have a scientific record that you can compare to another observation on a different day or to one made by someone else.

5 If you have a camera, try to take a picture of a whale. Show it to someone later and see if they know what it is. Tell them about the whale. Now you are a Whale Ambassador, spreading the word and helping other people learn about these great animals!

Some whales move from place to place, depending on the season. If you spend time at places where whales live, at the season when they are there, your patience might be rewarded with the sight of a living giant.

FACTS AT A GLANCE

⬇ *A humpback whale mom, her one-year-old calf, and research assistant Jason Sturgis swim together in the blue waters of Hawaii.*

Scientific Name

People use common names to refer to whales, but these can differ around the world. Scientists try to use the same name to refer to a species, no matter where they are. This is called its scientific name. For example, scientists call the humpback whale *Megaptera novaeangliae*. Whales, porpoises, and dolphins belong to a group of mammals called cetaceans.

Types of Whales

Whales are either toothed (Odontocetes) or baleen (Mysticetes). There are roughly 60–70 different species of toothed whales, porpoises, and dolphins, and 10–13 species of baleen whales. The largest whale, the blue whale, can be 100 feet (30 m) long and weigh 100-200 tons (91,000–181,000 kg). The smallest, the dwarf sperm whale, is about 8 feet long (2.5 m) and weighs about 900 pounds (400 kg).

Lifespans

Scientists don't really know how long whales can live. Some species of large whales may live more than 150 years.

Food

Toothed whales eat fish and squid. They sometimes blow a net of bubbles to trap the fish. Some whales use echolocation to bounce sound waves off their prey. They also stun fish with a blast of sound. Baleen whales scoop up water and food, and strain it through their baleen. They swallow the tiny animals left in their mouths.

Habitat and Range

Whales live in every ocean. Some, like pilot whales, live only in warm waters, while others, like narwhals, live only in the polar regions. Some species travel great distances. Gray whales have the longest migration of any mammal, 12,000 miles.

Behavior

Whales are some of Earth's most intelligent animals. They often live in family groups and spend time playing and swimming together. Curious whales sometimes approach boats.

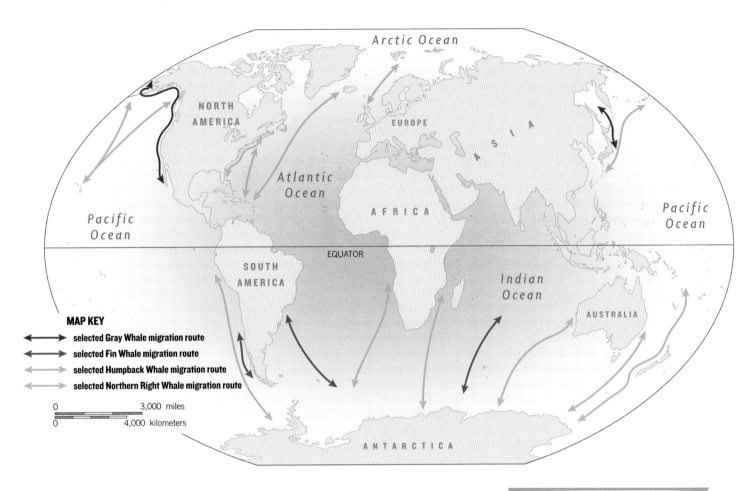

Whales live in all the world's oceans. Some whales travel long distances between summer feeding grounds and winter breeding grounds. This is called migration. Some selected whale migration routes are shown above.

MAP KEY

◄——►	selected Gray Whale migration route
◄——►	selected Fin Whale migration route
◄——►	selected Humpback Whale migration route
◄——►	selected Northern Right Whale migration route

0   3,000 miles
0   4,000 kilometers

Some whales communicate using whale "songs": squeaks, chirps, rumbles, and moans that can travel for hundreds of miles. Other whale behaviors include breaching (jumping high out of the water and then falling back), lobtailing (slapping the water with their tails or fins), and spyhopping (poking their heads above the surface to look around).

▬▬ Biggest threats

Pollution, overfishing, and climate change can wipe out whales' food. Some whales, even endangered species, are still being hunted. Other threats are commercial shipping (boats can hurt whales), noise pollution (underwater noise can confuse whales, possibly causing them to "strand," or swim up onto beaches), and oil slicks.

GLOSSARY

Aquarium: A park or attraction that specializes in animals and plants that live in the water.

Baleen: Long fringes or plates that some whales have in their mouths. Baleen whales strain out water and trap the tiny animals that they eat.

Breach: A behavior in which a whale leaps high out of the water and then falls back.

Cetacean: The name for the group of animals that includes whales, porpoises, and dolphins.

Echolocation: An adaptation that helps whales find food and find their way in the ocean. Toothed whales echolocate by sending out sounds and then listening to the echoes that bounce back. Bats and a few other species also echolocate.

Extinct: When the last member of a species dies out.

Forage: To look for food.

Habitat: The local environment in which an animal lives.

Krill: Tiny sea creatures that look like shrimp. Among the smallest animals in the world, they are food for whales, some of the largest animals!

Mammal: Air-breathing, warm-blooded animals with hair. whose offspring nurse on their mother's milk.

Marine mammal: A mammal that lives in or is dependent on the sea or ocean. Whales are marine mammals.

Migration: A long journey that some animals make, usually every year when the seasons change, to find food or other resources.

Pollution: Waste, garbage, and other undesirable things that make the water, air, or land dirty.

Species: A group of animals or plants that look similar, that can breed with one another, and whose offspring can also breed successfully.

Stranding: An event in which one or many whales get into very shallow water and wash up on a beach. Most stranded whales die.

Vertebrates: Animals that have a backbone.

FIND OUT MORE

Books & Articles

Carwardine, Mark, Erich Hoyt, R. Ewan Fordyce, Peter Gill. *Whales, Dolphins & Porpoises*. Alexandria, VA: Time-Life Books, 1998.

Dow, Lesley. *Whales* (Great Creatures of the World). New York, NY: Facts on File, Inc., 1990.

Whales & Dolphins (100 Things You Should Know About Series). New York, NY: Barnes & Noble Books, 2006.

Web Sites

American Cetacean Society fact pack pages at http://www.acsonline.org/factpack have detailed information about different species of whales and dolphins.

Hear beluga squeaks and chirps at the Interspecies.com site, http://www.interspecies.com/pages/beluga%20sound.html.

National Geographic Animal pages at http://animals.nationalgeographic.com. Animals have fact sheets and videos about animals from A to Z.

NOAA Fisheries has detailed Kids Pages about great whales at http://www.nmfs.noaa.gov/pr/education/whales.htm

Save the Whales at http://www.savethewhales.org/ has a mission to educate children and adults about marine mammals, their environment, and their preservation.

Whale Net at http://whale.wheelock.edu is an interactive educational Web site.

There are great photos of all kinds of whale behaviors at http://www.whalewatch.com/research/behaviors.php.

INDEX

Boldface *indicates illustrations.*

RESEARCH & PHOTOGRAPHIC NOTES

I keep my camera gear simple. I really like digital cameras. I shoot at high speeds, usually over a thousandth of a second. I'm usually in a boat, and I try to stay ready and hope whales will come close. I don't want to chase or scare the animals I am trying to photograph. I try to learn as much as I can about them and to respect them at all times. Whales are powerful and graceful, and they always leave me full of wonder, whether I take a picture or not.

My work depends on the researchers who dedicate themselves to learning about whales. Many of these people have spent decades in this pursuit, and as a result of their efforts we know a lot more than we did. But there is still much to learn. I hope some of the readers of this book will be inspired to continue scientific studies of the sea.

Some of my pictures are taken on whale-watching boats. The best whale watching operations follow the rules for working around whales and have good naturalists to help people understand what they are seeing.

Whales are very important to me, and I want to protect them. The Marine Mammal Protection Act makes it illegal to harass these animals. Most of my photos were made with researchers under special permits allowing them to work closely with whales with the understanding that the end product of their work will advance science and education. Having young readers know more and care more about whales is one of my goals in photographing whales.

Try to observe whales in their natural environment. You can see them from shore in some places, or from whale-watching boats or by volunteering with a research project. Be patient. As simple as it sounds, the more time you spend looking, the more you will see.

— FN

FOR OUR GRADE SCHOOL TEACH-
ERS, JIM CONBOY AND GORDON
PHIPPS, AND FOR ALL THOSE
TEACHERS WHO INSPIRE PEOPLE
TO EXPLORE AND CONTRIBUTE TO
THE WORLD — FN & LN

Acknowledgments:
We are very grateful to the researchers
who have shared their boats, camps,
experience, and discoveries. They are
completely responsible for these photo-
graphs being made. Jim Darling (Whale
Trust), Hal Whitehead (Dalhousie
University), Bruce Mate (Hatfield Marine
Science Center, Oregon State University),
Richard Sears (Mingan Island Cetacean
Study), and Jonathan Stern (San
Francisco State) are just a few of those
who have led the way. NATIONAL
GEOGRAPHIC magazine and Senior Editor
Kathy Moran have had an immeasurable
influence on our work with whales.
Thanks also to Douglas Chadwick, who
shared many of the adventures and who
inspires with his writing. Thank you all.

The publisher gratefully acknowledges
the assistance of Christine Kiel, K–3
curriculum and reading consultant; and
Bruce Mate (Director, Hatfield Marine
Science Center, Oregon State University)
for his assistance with the whale
migration map.

Photographs by Flip Nicklin/Minden
Pictures. Close photographs of humpback
whales taken under NMFS permit #753.

Book design by David M. Seager.
The body text of the book is set in
ITC Century. The display text is set
in Knockout and Party Noid.

Published by the
National Geographic Society

John M. Fahey, Jr., *President and*
Chief Executive Officer

Gilbert M. Grosvenor,
Chairman of the Board

Nina D. Hoffman, *Executive Vice*
President; President, Book
Publishing Group

Staff for This Book

Nancy Laties Feresten, *Vice President,*
Editor-in-Chief, Children's Books

Bea Jackson, *Design and Illustrations*
Director, Children's Books

Jennifer Emmett, Mary Beth Oelkers-
Keegan, *Project Editors*

David M. Seager, *Art Director*

Lori Epstein, *Illustrations Editor*

Jocelyn Lindsay, *Researcher*

Jean Cantu, *Illustrations Specialist*

Carl Mehler, *Director of Maps*

Rebecca Baines, *Editorial Assistant*

J. Naomi Linzer, *Indexer*

Jennifer Thornton, *Managing Editor*

R. Gary Colbert, *Production Director*

Lewis R. Bassford, *Production Manager*

Maryclare Tracy, Nicole Elliott,
Manufacturing Managers

Susan E. Borke, *Senior Vice President*
and Deputy General Counsel

Front cover: Face to face with a
humpback whale
Front flap: Part of a pod of whales in
the Atlantic, this sperm whale bares its
teeth as it surfaces.
Back cover: A sperm whale waves its
fluke, or tail.

Library of Congress
Cataloging-in-Publication Data

Nicklin, Flip.
  Face to face with whales / by Flip and
  Linda Nicklin.
    p. cm.—(Face to face with animals)
  Includes bibliographical references and
  index.
  ISBN 978-1-4263-0244-2 (trade: alk.
  paper)—ISBN 978-1-4263-0245-9 (library:
  alk. paper)
  1. Whales. 2. Whales—Pictorial works. I.
Nicklin, Linda. II. Title.
QL737.C4N476 2008
599.5--dc22

                              2007034249

Founded in 1888, the National Geographic
Society is one of the largest nonprofit
scientific and educational organizations in the
world. It reaches more than 285 million people worldwide each month through its official
journal, NATIONAL GEOGRAPHIC, and its four
other magazines; the National Geographic
Channel; television documentaries; radio pro-
grams; films; books; videos and DVDs; maps;
and interactive media. National Geographic
has funded more than 8,000 scientific
research projects and supports an education
program combating geographic illiteracy.

For more information, please call
1-800-NGS LINE (647-5463)
or write to the following address:

National Geographic Society
1145 17th Street N.W.
Washington, D.C. 20036-4688 U.S.A.

Visit us online at
www.nationalgeographic.com/books

For information about special discounts
for bulk purchases, please contact
National Geographic Books Special Sales:
ngspecsales@ngs.org

Printed in China